# ENTERTAINING

## SEAFOOD CHOWDER

1 lb (455 g) frozen haddock
2 tbs (30 ml) butter
1 large onion, chopped
3 stalks celery, chopped
3 carrots, chopped
3 potatoes, sliced
½ cup (120 ml) flour
½ tsp (3 ml) salt
2 tbs (30 ml) OLD BAY Seasoning
2 - 10¾ oz cans (645 ml)
    undiluted chicken broth
3 cups (720 ml) milk
1 - 8 oz pkg. (240 g) small shrimp
1½ lbs (685 g) sea legs, chopped
    (imitation crab meat)
1 cup (240 ml) cheddar cheese,
    grated

Thaw fish enough to cut into cubes. In large saucepan, melt butter and add vegetables; cook until onions are transparent. Blend in flour, salt, OLD BAY Seasoning. Cook for 1 minute, stirring constantly. Add chicken broth and milk and cook over medium heat for 25 minutes. Add haddock, shrimp, and sea legs and cook for an additional 10 minutes. Add cheese and cook until cheese is melted. Serve hot. Serves 8.

*Approximate nutritional analysis per serving:*
*Calories 388, Protein 39 g,*
*Carbohydrates 24 g, Fat 15 g,*
*Cholesterol 151 mg, Sodium 616 mg*

**Opposite: Seafood Chowder**

## CHICKEN BROCCOLI TRIANGLES

1½ lbs (685 g) (8–10 pieces)
    PREMIUM YOUNG 'N
    TENDER Brand Boneless,
    Skinless Chicken Thighs
2 tbs (30 ml) oil
¼ tsp (1 ml) crushed red pepper
1 clove garlic, minced
1 - 10 oz pkg. (300 g) frozen
    chopped broccoli, thawed
1 - 10¾ oz can (320 ml)
    condensed cream of chicken
    mushroom soup
¾ cup (180 ml) Parmesan cheese,
    grated
½ cup (120 ml) fresh cilantro,
    chopped
12 sheets phyllo pastry, thawed
1¼ cups (295 ml) butter or
    margarine, melted

Chop chicken thighs into very small pieces or grind in food processor. Heat oil in large skillet and sauté chicken, red pepper, and garlic over medium heat until done. Drain; set aside to cool. When cool, add broccoli, soup, cheese, and cilantro. Refrigerate until thoroughly chilled.

Work with 1 sheet of phyllo dough at a time, keeping others covered with plastic wrap to prevent drying out. Place 1 sheet on dry work surface with short edge toward you. Brush with melted butter. Fold bottom up about 3 inches. Cut dough vertically into 6 even strips. Place 1 full tsp of chicken filling at the bottom of each strip. Fold into a triangle, folding alternately to the right and to the left until entire strip of dough is used. Repeat with remaining dough and filling. Brush tops of each triangle with butter and place on 15x10x1-inch ungreased baking sheet. Bake in preheated 375°F (190°C) oven for 15–20 minutes or until golden brown. Can be served hot or cold. Yields 72 triangles.

Note: May be prepared ahead and frozen, up to 1 month. To cook, remove from freezer. Let stand 10 minutes to thaw and bake as above. May also be cooked under oven broiler.

*Approximate nutritional analysis per triangle:*
*Calories 61, Protein 3 g,*
*Carbohydrates 1 g, Fat 5 ,*
*Cholesterol 19 mg, Sodium 94 mg*

**Chicken
Broccoli Triangles**

# CHEESY TURKEY SAUSAGE BITES

**1 lb (455 g) bulk turkey sausage**
**3 cups (720 ml) BISQUICK**
**Reduced Fat baking mix**
**2 cups (8 oz) (240 g) reduced fat**
**cheddar cheese, shredded**
**½ cup (120 ml) green onions,**
**chopped**
**1 tsp (5 ml) dry mustard**
**½ tsp (3 ml) ground red pepper**
**(cayenne)**
**¾ cup (180 ml) skim milk**

**HONEY-MUSTARD SAUCE:**
**1 cup (240 ml) Dijon mustard**
**¼ cup (60 ml) honey**

Heat oven to 350°F (180°C). Cook and stir sausage in 10-inch skillet until brown, crumbling sausage into small bits; drain on paper towel. Mix sausage, baking mix, cheese, onions, mustard, and red pepper thoroughly in large bowl. Stir in milk. Drop dough by rounded teaspoonfuls about 2 inches apart onto ungreased cookie sheet. Bake about 15 minutes or until golden brown. Serve hot with Honey-Mustard Sauce. Yields 6 dozen appetizers.

Honey-Mustard Sauce: Stir mustard and honey in small bowl until blended. Yields 1¼ cups sauce.

*Approximate nutritional analysis per 4-bite serving: Calories 50, Protein 2 g, Carbohydrates 5 g, Fat 2 g, Cholesterol 5 mg, Sodium 150 mg*

# DRIED TOMATO PARTY POCKETS

**¼ cup (60 ml) SONOMA Dried**
**Tomato Bits**
**2 tbs (30 ml) boiling water**
**1 cup (4 oz) (120 g) sharp cheddar**
**cheese, shredded**
**3 tbs (45 ml) green onions, sliced**
**1 - 10 oz pkg. (300 g) prepared**
**refrigerated biscuits**
**1 egg, beaten**
**2 tsp (10 ml) sesame seeds**

Preheat oven to 400°F (205°C). In medium bowl mix tomato bits and water; set aside 5 minutes. Add cheese and onions; toss to blend evenly. On lightly floured surface, roll out each biscuit to a 4–5-inch circle. For each pocket, place about 2 tbs tomato mixture onto center of circle. Brush edge with egg. Fold over and press to seal completely. Place, spaced apart, on baking sheet. Brush with egg and sprinkle with sesame seeds. Bake 8–10 minutes until golden brown. Serve warm or at room temperature. Yields 10 pockets.

*Approximate nutritional analysis per serving: Calories 128, Protein 5 g, Carbohydrates 9 g, Fat 8 g, Cholesterol 35 mg, Sodium 224 mg*

***Dried Tomato Party Pockets***

## PEAR AND RICE VINAIGRETTE SALAD

**⅔ cup (160 ml) rice**
**1 - 6 oz jar (180 g) marinated artichoke hearts, halved**
**12 oz (360 g) small cooked shrimp**
**Lime Vinaigrette Dressing (below)**
**2 USA Pears, cored and diced**
**¼ cup (60 ml) Monterey Jack cheese, cubed**
**3 tbs (45 ml) green onions, sliced**
**2 tsp (10 ml) lime juice**
**radish roses and slices for garnish**
**USA Pear wedges for garnish**

**LIME VINAIGRETTE DRESSING:**
**vegetable oil**
**1 tbs (15 ml) lime juice**
**1 tbs (15 ml) vinegar**
**1 dash crushed dill weed**

Cook rice according to package directions until just tender. Drain artichoke hearts; reserve liquid for Lime Vinaigrette Dressing. Reserve 8–10 attractive whole shrimp for garnish. Combine hot rice, shrimp, and ¼ cup Lime Vinaigrette Dressing; let stand until cool. Combine pears, artichokes, cheese, onions, and lime juice with rice mixture; toss gently. Place rice mixture in deep 1½-qt mold or bowl such as small mixer bowl, or in 6 small custard cups. Refrigerate several hours or until thoroughly chilled. Unmold onto serving platter. Garnish top with reserved shrimp and radish slices. Garnish platter with pear wedges and radish roses. Serves 6.

Lime Vinaigrette Dressing: Add vegetable oil to reserved artichoke liquid to equal 3 tbs. Stir in lime juice, vinegar, and dill weed.

*Approximate nutritional analysis per serving:*
*Calories 234, Protein 14 g,*
*Carbohydrates 19 g, Fat 11 g,*
*Cholesterol 90 mg, Sodium 260 mg*

**Pear and Rice Vinaigrette Salad**

## WEST INDIES SEAFOOD SALAD

**SALAD:**
8 oz (240 g) large shrimp, cooked and peeled
8 oz (240 g) grouper or white fish filet, cubed and sautéed
½ medium purple onion, very thinly sliced
2 tsp (10 ml) capers, optional
2 tbs (30 ml) pineapple juice
1 tbs (15 ml) fresh lime juice
1 tbs (15 ml) olive oil
1 tsp (5 ml) McCORMICK or SCHILLING Chili Powder
½ ripe papaya, peeled and sliced
fresh pineapple slices, optional

**TROPICAL DRESSING:**
½ cup (120 ml) mayonnaise
¼ cup (60 ml) sour cream
¼ cup (60 ml) pineapple juice
2 tbs (30 ml) fresh lime juice
1 medium banana
1 tsp (5 ml) McCORMICK or SCHILLING Banana Extract

Salad: Combine all ingredients except fruit and toss. Marinate in refrigerator at least 2 hours. Serve mounded around fruit slices. Top with dressing. Serves 4.

Tropical Dressing: Process in a blender or mash banana and whip with other ingredients until creamy. Serves 4.

*Approximate nutritional analysis per serving salad: Calories 180, Protein 24 g, Carbohydrates 7 g, Fat 6 g, Cholesterol 104 mg, Sodium 116 mg*

*Approximate nutritional analysis per serving dressing: Calories 95, Protein < 1 g, Carbohydrates 10 g, Fat 7 g, Cholesterol 7 mg, Sodium 108 mg*

## SHRIMP SALAD WITH GRAPES

2 tbs (30 ml) salt
3 bay leaves
2 lbs (910 g) small or medium shrimp, shelled, uncooked
¾ cup (180 ml) celery, finely chopped
8 scallions, chopped
1½ tsp (8 ml) celery seed
1 tbs (15 ml) OLD BAY Seasoning, or more to taste
salt and freshly ground pepper to taste
2 cups (480 ml) mayonnaise
1 cup (240 ml) seedless green grapes
1 tbs (15 ml) capers, optional

Bring 4 quarts of water to a boil. Add salt and bay leaves. Add shrimp, cook for 1 minute, then pour into a colander. Cool. Chop shrimp to desired size, place in a large bowl, and toss with celery, scallions, celery seed, Old Bay Seasoning, salt, and pepper. Add mayonnaise, grapes, and capers (if desired). Cool salad in refrigerator for several hours. Adjust seasonings before serving. Serves 8.

*Approximate nutritional analysis per serving: Calories 365, Protein 24 g, Carbohydrates 19 g , Fat 22 g, Cholesterol 188 mg, Sodium 596 mg*

## ROASTY TOASTY SPINACH AND CHICK PEA SALAD

2 lbs (910 g) cleaned fresh spinach
2 small red onions, sliced thin
8 oz (240 g) mushrooms, cleaned and sliced
8 oz (240 g) cooked bacon, crumbled
¼ cup (60 ml) whole walnuts
4 oz (120 g) feta cheese, crumbled
1 - 16 oz can (480 g) GOYA Chick Peas, drained and rinsed
2 hard-boiled eggs, chopped

**WALNUT DRESSING:**
3 cloves garlic, minced
¼ cup (60 ml) cider vinegar
2 tbs (30 ml) wine mustard
1 cup (240 ml) GOYA Olive Oil
1 tsp (5 ml) GOYA Adobo
¾ cup (180 ml) crushed walnuts

In large salad bowl, toss all salad ingredients together. In small bowl, combine dressing ingredients and stir vigorously. Pour dressing over salad, toss, and serve. Serves 8.

*Approximate nutritional analysis per serving salad: Calories 294, Protein 17 g, Carbohydrates 18 g, Fat 18 g, Cholesterol 77 mg, Sodium 660 mg*

*Approximate nutritional analysis per ¼ cup serving dressing: Calories 316, Protein 2 g, Carbohydrates 3 g, Fat 34 g, Cholesterol 0 mg, Sodium 117 mg*

## OLD BAY NOODLES AND CRAB

**4 tbs (60 ml) butter or margarine**
**1 lb (455 g) lump crab meat,**
  **cooked**
**1 tsp (5 ml) OLD BAY Seasoning,**
  **or more to taste**
**¾ cup (180 ml) half-and-half**
**¼ cup (60 ml) sherry**
**3 egg yolks, beaten**
**1 lb (455 g) broad noodles,**
  **cooked and drained**

In a medium saucepan, heat butter.
Add cooked crab meat and Old Bay
Seasoning. Cook at medium until very
hot. Pour in half-and-half and bring to
a boil; add sherry. Pour some of the hot
liquid slowly into egg yolks while
beating vigorously. Return to the crab
mixture. Cook until sauce is thickened;
do not boil. Mix with cooked noodles.
Serve hot. Serves 4.

*Approximate nutritional analysis per serving:*
*Calories 705, Protein 40 g,*
*Carbohydrates 87 g, Fat 19 g,*
*Cholesterol 303 mg, Sodium 451 mg*

## CHICKEN AND TWO-PEPPER PASTA

**¼ cup (60 ml) LAND O LAKES**
  **Sweet Cream Butter**
**½ cup (120 ml) chopped onion**
**1 tsp (5 ml) finely chopped fresh**
  **garlic**
**½ medium yellow pepper,**
  **cut into thin strips**
**½ medium red pepper,**
  **cut into thin strips**
**3 boneless chicken breast halves,**
  **skinned, cut into 3x½-inch**
  **strips**
**½ tsp (3 ml) salt**
**¼ tsp (1 ml) coarsely ground**
  **pepper**
**6 oz (180 g) dried spinach**
  **fettuccine, cooked and**
  **drained**
**¾ cup (180 ml) half-and-half**
**1 cup (4 oz) (120 g) shredded**
  **LAND O LAKES Mozzarella**
  **Cheese**
**¼ cup (60 ml) freshly grated**
  **Parmesan cheese**

In 10-inch skillet, melt butter until
sizzling. Stir in onion, garlic, and
peppers. Cook over medium-high heat
until vegetables are crisply tender,
2–3 minutes. Spoon vegetables from
pan, reserving juices in pan. Set
vegetables aside; keep warm. In same
skillet add chicken to reserved juices.
Continue cooking, stirring occasionally,
until chicken is browned and fork
tender, 7–9 minutes. Reduce heat to
low. Add salt and pepper. Add cooked
fettuccine, vegetables, and half-and-
half; continue cooking, stirring
constantly, until heated through, 3–5
minutes. Add mozzarella cheese and
2 tbs Parmesan cheese; continue
cooking, stirring constantly, until
mozzarella cheese is melted, 1–2
minutes. Sprinkle with remaining
Parmesan cheese; serve immediately.
Serves 4.

*Approximate nutritional analysis per serving:*
*Calories 375, Protein 28 g,*
*Carbohydrates 24 g, Fat 18 g,*
*Cholesterol 90 mg, Sodium 486 mg*

***Opposite:***
***Chicken and Two-Pepper Pasta***

## ELEGANT CHICKEN LASAGNE

3 lbs (1.4 kg) PREMIUM YOUNG
   'N TENDER Brand Boneless,
   Skinless, Split Chicken
   Breasts, cut into bite size
   pieces
3 tbs (45 ml) olive oil
½ cup (120 ml) butter
⅓ cup (80 ml) all-purpose flour
4 cups (960 ml) milk
1 tsp (5 ml) salt
½ tsp (3 ml) ground white pepper
½ cup (120 ml) crumbled Stilton
   cheese, or blue cheese
2 tbs (30 ml) dry white wine
8 oz (240 g) grated Muenster
   cheese
8 oz (240 g) grated provolone
   cheese
8 oz (240 g) grated white cheddar
   cheese
1 lb (455 g) lasagne noodles,
   cooked al dente, drained well
3 large firm ripe tomatoes,
   peeled, seeded, and chopped
½ cup (120 ml) chopped fresh
   basil leaves *or* 2 tsp (10 ml)
   dried basil leaves
½ lb (230 g) fresh mushrooms,
   thinly sliced
fresh basil leaves, optional

Preheat oven to 350°F (180°C). Lightly butter a 13x9x2-inch baking dish; set aside.

Sauté chicken in heated olive oil in a large skillet over moderately high heat until done, about 5 minutes. If necessary, cook in several batches. Remove with a slotted spoon; set aside.

Melt butter in a medium saucepan over moderately low heat. Add flour, cooking and stirring about 3 minutes. Whisk in milk. Continue cooking and stirring 8–10 minutes or until smooth and thickened. Remove sauce from heat; add salt, pepper, Stilton cheese, and white wine, stirring until cheese has melted. Set aside.

Combine Muenster, provolone, and cheddar cheese, mixing well. Set aside.

To assemble lasagne, spread an even layer of sauce in the prepared baking dish. Top with ⅓ of the noodles, ⅓ of the remaining sauce, and half of each of the following: tomatoes, basil, mushrooms, and chicken. Top with ⅓ of the cheese mixture. Repeat layering in the same manner. End with the remaining ⅓ of the noodles, sauce and cheese mixture.

Bake in center of the preheated oven for 50–60 minutes or until hot and bubbly. Let stand 10 minutes before serving. Garnish with basil leaves if desired. Serves 12.

Note: May be prepared ahead. Cover well; refrigerate or freeze and bake later.

*Approximate nutritional analysis per serving:*
*Calories 719, Protein 59 g,*
*Carbohydrates 37 g, Fat 37 g,*
*Cholesterol 183 mg, Sodium 849 mg*

## OLD BAY ONION PIE

3 tbs (45 ml) butter
6 medium onions, peeled and
   sliced
1 tsp (5 ml) OLD BAY Seasoning
¼ tsp (1 ml) salt
1½ cups (355 ml) milk
5 eggs, beaten
1 - 9-inch pie shell
2 tbs (30 ml) parsley
12 slices bacon, cooked, drained,
   and crumbled

Preheat oven to 350°F (180°C). In a medium saucepan, melt butter and sauté onions, Old Bay Seasoning, and salt over low heat for 15 minutes, stirring occasionally. Drain. Add milk and stir in eggs. Pour mixture in pie shell; top with parsley and bacon. Bake for 50 minutes until done. Serves 8.

*Approximate nutritional analysis per serving:*
*Calories 319, Protein 9 g,*
*Carbohydrates 32 g, Fat 18 g,*
*Cholesterol 26 mg, Sodium 429 mg*

# QUICK CHICKEN FAJITA PIZZA

**2 tsp (10 ml) olive or vegetable oil**

**2 whole chicken breasts, skinned, boned, cut into 2x½-inch strips**

**1–2 tsp (5–10 ml) McCORMICK chili powder**

**½ tsp (3 ml) salt**

**½ tsp (3 ml) McCORMICK garlic powder**

**1 cup (240 ml) onions, thinly sliced**

**1 cup (240 ml) green or red bell pepper strips, 2x¼-inch**

**1 - 10 oz can (300 g) refrigerated pizza crust**

**½ cup (120 ml) prepared mild salsa or picante sauce**

**4 oz (1 cup) (120 g) Monterey Jack cheese, shredded**

Heat oil in large skillet over medium-high heat until hot. Add chicken; cook and stir 5 minutes or until lightly browned. Stir in chili powder, salt, and garlic powder. Add onions and bell pepper; cook and stir an additional 1 minute or until vegetables are crisp-tender.

Heat oven to 425°F (220°C). Grease 12-inch pizza pan or 13x9-inch pan. Unroll dough; place in greased pan. Starting at center, press out with hands. Bake for 6–8 minutes or until very light golden brown. Spoon chicken mixture over partially baked crust, spoon salsa over chicken; sprinkle with cheese. Bake an additional 14–18 minutes or until crust is golden brown. Serves 8.

*Approximate nutritional analysis per serving:*
*Calories 260, Protein 21 g,*
*Carbohydrates 20 g, Fat 11 g,*
*Cholesterol 49 mg, Sodium 600 mg*

*Quick Chicken Fajita Pizza*

# TANDOORI-STYLE CHICKEN

1 cup (240 ml) DANNON Plain
    Nonfat or Lowfat Yogurt
3 tbs (45 ml) distilled white
    vinegar
2 tsp (10 ml) minced garlic
1¾ tsp (9 ml) garam masala*
1¼ tsp (6 ml) ground ginger
¼ tsp (1 ml) ground red pepper
6 boneless skinless chicken
    breast halves, trimmed of all
    visible fat
1¼ tsp (6 ml) salt
3 tsp (15 ml) olive oil, divided
2 cups (480 ml) sliced onions

* Garam masala is available in most Indian specialty shops or make your own from common kitchen spices, listed below:

In small bowl, combine:
1½ tsp (8 ml) ground cumin
1 tsp (5 ml) ground coriander
1 tsp (5 ml) ground cardamom
1 tsp (5 ml) pepper
¼ tsp (1 ml) ground bay leaves
    (If ground bay leaves are not
    available, grind whole leaves
    to a fine powder with a
    mortar and pestle.)
pinch of ground cloves

In a large glass bowl combine yogurt, vinegar, garlic, garam masala, ginger, and red pepper. Cut 4 ½-inch-deep diagonal slashes in top of each chicken breast. Sprinkle salt in slashes. Add chicken to yogurt mixture. Cover; chill at least 8 hours or overnight.

Preheat oven to 375°F. Brush 13x9-inch baking dish with 1 tsp oil. Remove chicken from marinade and arrange in a single layer, cut side up, in baking dish. Spoon some of the marinade over chicken; discard remainder. Sprinkle onions over chicken and drizzle with remaining 2 tsp oil. Bake 25–30 minutes or until chicken is no longer pink. Place chicken under broiler 3–5 minutes to brown onions. Serve immediately. Serves 6.

*Approximate nutritional analysis per serving: Calories 283, Protein 44 g, Carbohydrates 8 g, Fat 8 g, Cholesterol 115 mg, Sodium 570 mg*

# CHICKEN CREOLE

1 cup (240 ml) CALIFORNIA
    Ripe Olives, in wedges
1 cup (240 ml) frozen peas
1 tsp (5 ml) brown sugar
¼ tsp (1 ml) cinnamon
½ tsp (3 ml) garlic salt
¼ tsp (1 ml) black pepper
1 tsp (5 ml) hot pepper sauce
2 cups (480 ml) quick-cooking
    rice
1 tbs (15 ml) olive oil
½ cup (120 ml) diced onion
1 cup (240 ml) diced green
    pepper
½ tsp (3 ml) turmeric
1¾ cups (415 ml) tomato juice
1 lb (455 g) skinless chicken
    breasts

Combine first seven ingredients in small bowl. Measure rice into small bowl. Mix olive oil, onion, and green pepper in 12x8-inch glass baking dish. Microwave on HIGH for 3 minutes. Add all ingredients except chicken. Stir well. Place chicken breasts on top. Cover with plastic wrap. Microwave on HIGH for 10 minutes. Turn chicken over. Rotate dish ¼ turn. Cover with plastic wrap. Microwave on HIGH until chicken is cooked, about 7–10 more minutes. Serves 6.

*Approximate nutritional analysis per serving: Calories 436, Protein 30 g, Carbohydrates 61 g, Fat 7 g, Cholesterol 64 mg, Sodium 530 mg*

*Opposite: Chicken Creole*

## SAUCY HERBED CHICKEN BREASTS

**2 tbs (30 ml) margarine or butter**
**2 tbs (30 ml) shortening or vegetable oil**
**4 chicken breasts, cut in half**
**½ cup (120 ml) finely chopped onion**
**1 large clove garlic, finely chopped**
**4 oz (120 g) mushrooms, sliced**
**¼ cup (60 ml) margarine or butter**
**¾ cup (180 ml) dry white wine**
**3 tbs (45 ml) cornstarch**
**¼ cup (60 ml) water**
**2 cups (480 ml) YOPLAIT Fat Free Plain Yogurt**
**1 tsp (5 ml) salt**
**½ tsp (3 ml) dried tarragon leaves**

Heat oven to 350°F (180°C). Heat 2 tbs margarine and the shortening in rectangular baking dish, 13x9x2 inches, in oven until melted. Place chicken in dish; turn to coat with margarine mixture. Arrange chicken, skin sides up, in dish. Bake uncovered 1 hour; drain.

Cook onion, garlic, and mushrooms in ¼ cup margarine in 10-inch skillet until onion is tender; stir in wine. Stir cornstarch into water until smooth; stir into wine mixture. Heat to boiling, stirring constantly. Boil and stir 1 minute; remove from heat. Stir in yogurt, salt, and tarragon leaves; pour over chicken. Cover tightly with aluminum foil. Bake 10–15 minutes longer or until chicken is done. Remove chicken to warm platter. Stir sauce; spoon over chicken. Sprinkle with additional tarragon leaves if desired. Serves 8.

High altitude (3500–6500 ft): Increase first bake time to 1½ hours.

*Approximate nutritional analysis per serving:*
*Calories 240, Protein 27 g,*
*Carbohydrates 10 g, Fat 10 g,*
*Cholesterol 65 mg, Sodium 440 mg*

## GARLIC LOVER'S CHICKEN

**2 EMPIRE KOSHER Fryers, cut into serving pieces, skin removed**
**40 cloves garlic (3–4 heads), peeled but left whole**
**¼ cup (60 ml) olive oil**
**4 stalks of celery, cut into 1-inch strips**
**2 tbs (30 ml) parsley**
**1 tbs (15 ml) tarragon**
**¼ tsp (1 ml) nutmeg**
**salt and pepper**
**⅓ cup (80 ml) kosher cognac or white wine**

Place garlic in 5-qt casserole and cook in microwave on HIGH for 3 minutes. Add olive oil, celery, parsley, tarragon, and nutmeg. Stir well. Season chicken with salt and pepper. Place in casserole and turn to coat well. Add cognac or wine and turn chicken in mixture again. Cover with plastic wrap and cook on high for 20 minutes, rearranging pieces after 10 minutes. Reduce setting to medium power, cook another 40 minutes, stirring every 15 minutes. Serve with French bread, dipped in the cooking juices. Serves 8.

*Approximate nutritional analysis per serving:*
*Calories 631, Protein 83 g,*
*Carbohydrates 6 g, Fat 28 g,*
*Cholesterol 251 mg, Sodium 263 mg*

## SWEDISH MEATBALLS

½ cup (120 ml) seltzer
    or soda water
½ cup (120 ml) kosher parve
    bread crumbs
1 lb (455 g) EMPIRE KOSHER
    Ground Turkey
1 lb (455 g) EMPIRE KOSHER
    Ground Chicken
2 onions, grated
2 eggs
salt and pepper to taste
2 tbs (30 ml) margarine
1 tbs (15 ml) vegetable oil

Soak the bread crumbs in seltzer or soda water for 15 minutes. Leftover mashed potatoes may be used rather than bread crumbs. Mix with ground meats, add the grated onion and the eggs. Mix briefly. Do not overmix or meatballs will be tough. Wet hands, roll meatballs between the palms of your hands to about the size of large walnuts. Place on lightly oiled plate. Melt margarine in heavy skillet, add a little vegetable oil. Over medium heat, add meatballs to pan, shaking constantly so that meatballs turn and brown on all sides while keeping their shape. Do not overcrowd. Serve with mashed potatoes, green beans, and cranberry sauce, as the Swedes do. Serves 4.

*Approximate nutritional analysis per serving:*
*Calories 607, Protein 67 g,*
*Carbohydrates 20 g, Fat 27 g,*
*Cholesterol 285 mg, Sodium 318 mg*

**Swedish Meatballs**

## GRILLED ITALIAN STEAK

¾ cup (180 ml) WISH-BONE
    Italian, Robusto Italian,
    or Lite Italian Dressing
2 tbs (30 ml) grated Parmesan
    cheese
2 tsp (10 ml) dried basil leaves,
    crushed
¼ tsp (1 ml) cracked black
    pepper
2–3 lbs (910–1365 g) boneless
    sirloin or London broil steak

In large shallow baking dish or plastic bag, combine all ingredients except steak; mix well. Add steak; turn to coat. Cover dish or close bag, and marinate in refrigerator, turning occasionally, 3 hours or overnight. Remove steak, reserving marinade. Grill or broil steak until done. Meanwhile, in small saucepan, bring reserved marinade to a boil, then pour over steak. Serves 8.

*Approximate nutritional analysis per serving:
Calories 310, Protein 32 g,
Carbohydrates 3 g, Fat 19 g,
Cholesterol 75 mg, Sodium 560 mg*

## QUICK CHICKEN CACCIATORE

1 - 2½–3½ lb (1.1–1.6 kg)
    EMPIRE KOSHER
    Fryer Chicken
1 pkg. kosher parve onion
    soup mix
4 cups (960 ml) stewed tomatoes
¼ lb (60 ml) fresh mushrooms,
    sliced
½ tsp (3 ml) rosemary
½ tsp (3 ml) thyme

Cut the fryer in serving pieces; remove skin. Place in large microwave-safe casserole, add remaining ingredients. Cover with plastic wrap or wax paper. Cook on HIGH 20–25 minutes, turning dish at least once. Serve with noodles or brown rice. Serves 6.

    Conventional oven: Preheat oven to 325°F (165°C). Proceed as above, but do not cover. Bake for 1 hour or until juices run clear and chicken is tender.

*Approximate nutritional analysis per serving:
Calories 485, Protein 67 g,
Carbohydrates 5 g, Fat 17 g,
Cholesterol 201 mg, Sodium 665 mg*

*Grilled Italian Steak*

## MANDARIN STEAK STIR-FRY

⅔ cup (160 ml) chicken broth
2 tbs (30 ml) rice vinegar
4 tsp (20 ml) cornstarch
2 cloves fresh garlic, minced
1 tbs (15 ml) soy sauce
1 tsp (5 ml) McCORMICK or
    SCHILLING Pure Orange
    Extract
1 tbs (15 ml) sesame oil
2 tsp (10 ml) vegetable oil
12 oz (360 g) beef, cut in
    ½-inch strips
1 cup (240 ml) frozen baby
    carrots
1 medium golden or red bell
    pepper, cut into ¼-inch strips
1 - 5 oz can (150 g) sliced water
    chestnuts, drained
1 cup (240 ml) snow peas,
    strings removed
2 tbs (30 ml) minced fresh ginger

Mix chicken broth, vinegar, cornstarch, garlic, soy sauce, and orange extract. Set aside. In large skillet, heat sesame and vegetable oils over medium-high heat. When hot, add beef strips and stir-fry 30 seconds. Remove to platter and hold. In the same skillet, add frozen carrots and cook 1 minute. Add remaining ingredients and stir-fry 2 minutes. Add liquid mixture and stir-fry about 4 minutes or until sauce has thickened. Add beef, toss well, and serve over rice or cellophane noodles. Pass soy sauce at the table if desired. Serves 4.

*Approximate nutritional analysis per serving:*
*Calories 283, Protein 28 g,*
*Carbohydrates 14 g, Fat 13 g,*
*Cholesterol 76 mg, Sodium 411 mg*

## WONDERFULLY QUICK BEEF TENDERLOIN

nonstick vegetable oil spray
1 - 5¾ lb (2.6 kg) whole beef
    tenderloin, trimmed,
    preferably heavy aged beef*
3 tbs (45 ml) extra virgin olive oil
2 tbs (30 ml) CHEF PAUL
    PRUDHOMME'S Blackened
    Steak Magic

* Ask your butcher to trim the tenderloin. If you want to trim it yourself, remove all the silver skin from the meat. Then remove the back strap: To find it, lay the tenderloin down with the larger end to your right; the back strap is on the back side of the tenderloin and is immediately evident when you remove the silver skin. It can be removed with your fingers. Don't remove the marbled fat from the bottom side; it will keep the tenderloin from sticking to the pan. The trimmings can be browned off and used for gravy.

Spray a heavy roasting pan (without rack) with vegetable spray. Place the tenderloin in the roasting pan, fat side down. Pour the olive oil directly in the pan and use it to oil the tenderloin really well. The three tbs will coat the meat and leave enough remaining to coat the pan. This is necessary because the tenderloin has so little fat on it.

Sprinkle the Blackened Steak Magic lightly and evenly over the tenderloin—on every surface—and pat it in. Refrigerate the tenderloin and baking pan for 1 hour. Don't remove it from the refrigerator until you're ready to place it in the oven. It's important for the tenderloin to be cold when you place it in the hot oven.

While the meat is chilling, preheat the oven to 550°F (288°C). Be sure to check your oven temperature with a free-standing oven thermometer to see if it registers accurately; most home ovens vary somewhat from the temperature you set.

Place roasting pan in the middle of the oven and bake until a probe inserted into the thickest part of the meat registers 127°F (53°C) for a true rare (cool red center), about 25 minutes. Increase the cooking time in very small increments to reach medium rare (138°F (59°C)), medium (148°F (64°C)), medium well (158°F (70°C)). Any temperature in excess of 165°F (74°C) is considered well done—but don't do this to a fine cut of beef. Remove from oven and transfer meat to a cutting board or platter; let sit 15–20 minutes. Carve and serve immediately. Serves 10.

*Approximate nutritional analysis per serving:*
*Calories 561, Protein 80 g,*
*Carbohydrates 0 g, Fat 25 g,*
*Cholesterol 232 mg, Sodium 279 mg*

# GRILLED LAMB KABOBS WITH COUSCOUS TABBOULEH

## COUSCOUS TABBOULEH:
½ cup (120 ml) couscous
¾ cup (180 ml) boiling water
2 medium tomatoes, coarsely chopped
⅓ cup (80 ml) chopped fresh parsley
¼ cup (60 ml) chopped green onion
3 tbs (45 ml) fresh lemon juice
1 tbs (15 ml) finely chopped fresh mint *or* ¼ tsp (1 ml) dried mint leaves, crushed
½ tsp (3 ml) salt
freshly ground black pepper, as desired

## GRILLED LAMB KABOBS:
1 medium onion, cut in half crosswise
2 tbs (30 ml) olive oil
2 cloves garlic, crushed
1 tsp (5 ml) dried basil leaves, crushed
¼ tsp (1 ml) ground cinnamon
1 lb (455 g) well-trimmed boneless lamb leg, cut into 1¼-inch pieces
1 small lemon, cut into 8 wedges
¼ cup (60 ml) apple jelly
2 tbs (30 ml) fresh lemon juice
1 tsp (5 ml) chopped fresh mint *or* ¼ tsp (1 ml) dried mint leaves, crushed

Couscous Tabbouleh: Combine couscous and boiling water; cover and let stand 5 minutes. Cool. Crumble couscous with fingers. Combine couscous, tomatoes, parsley, onion, lemon juice, mint, salt, and pepper in bowl. Serve at room temperature. Yields 3 cups.

Lamb Kabobs: Cut each onion half into quarters; separate into pieces. Combine oil, garlic, basil, and cinnamon. Place lamb leg pieces, onion, and lemon wedges in plastic bag; add marinade, turning to coat. Close bag securely and marinate in refrigerator 1 hour. Meanwhile combine apple jelly, lemon juice, and mint in small saucepan. Cook over low heat until jelly melts, stirring occasionally. Remove lamb cubes, onion and lemon from marinade; discard marinade. Alternately thread lamb cubes, onion pieces, and lemon wedges on each of four 12-inch metal skewers. Place kabobs on grill over medium coals. Grill 8–12 minutes for medium, turning and brushing with jelly mixture occasionally. Serve kabobs with Couscous Tabbouleh.  Serves 4.

*Approximate nutritional analysis per ¾ cup serving Couscous Tabbouleh: Calories 106, Protein 4 g, Carbohydrates 18 g, Fat < 1 g, Cholesterol 0 mg, Sodium 281 mg*

*Approximate nutritional analysis per kabob: Calories 280, Protein 23 g, Carbohydrates 18 g, Fat 13 g, Cholesterol 79 mg, Sodium 83 mg*

# PEPPERED PORK ROAST

2–4 lb (910–1820 g) boneless pork roast
1–2 tsp (5–10 ml) garlic pepper
1–2 tsp (5–10 ml) dried rosemary, crushed

Coat roast with seasoning mixture of garlic pepper and rosemary. Place roast in a shallow pan in a preheated 350°F (180°C) oven for 45 minutes–1½ hours, until meat thermometer inserted registers 155°F (68°C). Remove from oven and let roast rest for 5–10 minutes before slicing to serve. Serves 6.

*Approximate nutritional analysis per serving: Calories 167, Protein 24 g, Fat 6 g, Cholesterol 66 mg, Sodium 78 mg*

Courtesy of the National Pork Producers Council.

*Opposite:*
***Grilled Lamb Kabobs
with Couscous Tabbouleh***

## SUMMER SWISS STEAK

**8 oz (240 g) shitake mushrooms
   or button mushrooms**
**1½ lbs (685 g) boneless veal
   round steak, cut ½-inch thick**
**1 tbs (15 ml) olive oil**
**salt and freshly ground black
   pepper to taste**
**⅓ cup (80 ml) dry white wine**
**2 medium tomatoes, seeded and
   diced**
**⅓ cup (80 ml) thinly sliced fresh
   basil leaves**

Cut small mushrooms in half, large mushrooms into quarters; reserve. Cut veal round steak into six pieces. Pound steak pieces to ⅛-inch thickness. Heat oil in 12-inch non-stick skillet. Brown veal pieces, a few at a time; remove and keep warm. Return all veal to skillet; season with salt and pepper to taste. Cook, uncovered, over medium heat 4–5 minutes or until tender, turning occasionally. Remove veal to platter; keep warm. Add wine and mushrooms to skillet, stirring to dissolve browned meat juices attached to pan. Cook over medium-high heat 3 minutes or until mushrooms are tender, stirring frequently. Add tomato and basil; heat through. Spoon vegetable mixture over veal. Serves 6.

Note: A veal round steak will yield 4 - 3 oz (360 g) cooked, trimmed servings per lb (455 g).

***Opposite: Spring Lamb Crown
Roast with Vegetable Stuffing***

*Approximate nutritional analysis per serving:
Calories 175, Protein 26 g,
Carbohydrates 5 g, Fat 5 g,
Cholesterol 91 mg, Sodium 263 mg*

Courtesy of the National Livestock and Meat Board.

## SPRING LAMB CROWN ROAST WITH VEGETABLE STUFFING

**3–3½ lb (1.4–1.6 kg), 14–16-rib
   lamb crown roast**
**3 tbs (45 ml) butter or margarine**
**1 medium onion, chopped**
**1 large green bell pepper,
   cut into thin strips**
**8 oz (240 g) mushrooms, coarsely
   chopped**
**1 large clove garlic, crushed**
**3 - 10 oz pkgs. ( 900 g) frozen
   chopped spinach, defrosted,
   drained well**
**¾ tsp (4 ml) salt**
**⅛ tsp (.5 ml) pepper**

Place lamb crown roast, rib ends down, on rack in shallow roasting pan. Do not add water. Do not cover. Roast in moderate, 375°F (190°C), oven 20 minutes. Meanwhile melt butter in large skillet. Add onion; cook 4–5 minutes or until onion is transparent, stirring occasionally. Add bell pepper, mushrooms, and garlic; continue cooking 5 minutes, stirring occasionally. Stir in spinach, salt, and pepper. Remove roast from oven. Turn roast so rib ends are up. Insert meat thermometer into thickest part of roast, not touching bone or fat. Fill cavity of roast with spinach stuffing. Continue roasting 25–35 minutes or until meat thermometer registers 135°F (57°C) for rare to 155°F (68°C) for medium. Cover roast with aluminum foil tent and allow to stand 10–15 minutes. Roast will continue to rise approximately 5°F (3°C) in temperature to reach 140°F (60°C) for rare and 160°F (71°C) for medium. Trim excess fat from roast; carve roast between ribs. Serves 5-7.

Note: A lamb crown roast will yield 1½–2 - 3 oz (150-180 g) cooked, trimmed servings per lb (455 g).

*Approximate nutritional analysis per serving:
Calories 656, Protein 33 g,
Carbohydrates 10 g, Fat 54 g,
Cholesterol 147 mg, Sodium 484 mg*

Courtesy of the National Livestock and Meat Board.

***Summer Swiss Steak***

## SWEET AND SOUR CRAB PATTIES

**1 lb (455 g) crab meat, picked**
**½ lb (230 g) ground turkey**
**1 green onion, chopped**
**2 tsp (10 ml) OLD BAY Seasoning**
**1 egg white**
**2 tsp (10 ml) cornstarch**
**1 cup (240 ml) flour**
**½ cup (120 ml) vegetable oil**

**SWEET AND SOUR SAUCE:**
**1½ cups (355 ml) water**
**2 tbs (30 ml) cornstarch**
**2 tbs (30 ml) catsup**
**2 tbs (30 ml) soy sauce**
**½ cup (120 ml) packed brown sugar**
**½ cup (120 ml) apple cider vinegar**

Patties: In a large bowl, blend crab meat, turkey, onion, Old Bay Seasoning, egg white, and cornstarch. Shape 24 patties and dust with flour. Set patties on wax paper and chill while making the sauce.

In wok or heavy skillet, heat vegetable oil, and cook patties over high heat. Serve patties with Sweet and Sour Sauce. Serves 24.

Sweet and Sour Sauce: In a bowl, whisk together water and cornstarch until thoroughly blended. Stir in catsup, soy sauce, brown sugar, and vinegar. Bring to a boil in a saucepan, stirring until mixture thickens, about 1 minute. Remove from heat. Use hot or cold.

*Approximate nutritional analysis per patty plus 1 tbs sauce: Calories 124, Protein 7 g, Carbohydrates 10 g, Fat 6 g, Cholesterol 25 mg, Sodium 188 mg*

## SWEET AND SPICY ALMOND GREEN BEANS

**1 lb (455 g) green beans, cut into lengthwise strips**
**½ cup (120 ml) BLUE DIAMOND Chopped Natural Almonds**
**1 tbs (15 ml) vegetable oil**
**2 tbs (30 ml) butter**
**1 clove garlic, chopped finely**
**1 tbs (15 ml) firmly packed brown sugar**
**2–3 tsp (10–15 ml) lemon juice**
**¼ tsp (1 ml) red pepper flakes**
**¼ tsp (1 ml) salt**

*Opposite:*
*Sweet and Spicy*
*Almond Green Beans*

Plunge green beans into salted, boiling water. Cook until just tender, about 3–4 minutes. Drain and rinse in cold water. Sauté almonds in oil until crisp. Add butter to pan and add green beans. Stir to coat and heat. Stir in garlic, brown sugar, lemon juice, red pepper flakes, and salt. Cook, stirring constantly, until sugar dissolves and beans are glazed, about 30 seconds. Serves 6.

*Approximate nutritional analysis per serving: Calories 151, Protein 4 g, Carbohydrates 10 g, Fat 12 g, Cholesterol 10 mg, Sodium 96 mg*

*Sweet and Sour*
*Crab Patties*

## ALMOND-RAISIN PILAF

⅔ cup (160 ml) BLUE DIAMOND
    Blanched Slivered Almonds
3 tbs (45 ml) butter, divided
1 cup (240 ml) chopped onion
2 cloves garlic, chopped finely
1 small, green bell pepper, diced
1 cup (240 ml) long-grain rice
½ cup (120 ml) raisins
1 tsp (5 ml) cumin
½ tsp (3 ml) salt
1¾ cups (415 ml) chicken broth

Sauté almonds in 1 tbs butter until golden; reserve. Sauté onion and garlic in remaining 2 tbs butter until translucent. Add green pepper, rice, raisins, cumin, and salt; sauté 2 minutes. Add chicken broth. Bring to a boil. Reduce heat to low, cover, and cook 20 minutes or until all liquid is absorbed. Remove from heat and let stand, covered, 5 minutes. Stir in almonds. Serves 6.

*Approximate nutritional analysis per serving: Calories 302, Protein 6 g, Carbohydrates 41 g, Fat 14 g, Cholesterol 16 mg, Sodium 277 mg*

**Almond-Raisin Pilaf**

## MEDITERRANEAN ROASTED VEGETABLE AND CHEESE CASSEROLE

2 large onions, cut into narrow
    wedges
2 lb (910 g) zucchini, sliced
¼ cup (60 ml) olive oil
¼ cup (60 ml) flour
1 lb (455 g) tomatoes, cut into
    wedges
2 red bell peppers, cut into
    squares
½ cup (120 ml) pine nuts
1 cup (240 ml) CALIFORNIA
    Ripe Olives, halved
⅓ cup (80 ml) minced fresh basil
1 cup (240 ml) grated fontina
    or other medium-soft cheese
¼ cup (60 ml) balsamic vinegar

Sauté onions and zucchini in oil until tender. Turn into wide, shallow baking dish that holds about 3 qts. Sprinkle with flour. Arrange tomatoes and bell peppers on top. Bake uncovered at 450°F (230°C) for 20 minutes or until fork-tender. Top with pine nuts and olives, then basil, then cheese. Bake 10–12 minutes longer. Drizzle with balsamic vinegar before serving. Serves 6.

*Approximate nutritional analysis per serving: Calories 354, Protein 13 g, Carbohydrates 27 g, Fat 25 g, Cholesterol 22 mg, Sodium 291 mg*